The Way Things Were

EDWARDIAN
ENGLAND

Edited by Andrew Pagett

Illustrated by Contemporary Artists

BROCKHAMPTON PRESS

Edwardian England

First published by Brockhampton Press Ltd
20 Bloomsbury Street
London WC1B 3QA

© Brockhampton Press Ltd, 1999

ISBN 1 86019 944 5

Conceived and designed by Savitri Books Ltd

Printed and bound by
APP Printing, Singapore

049593

O My Mother Isle!
O native Britain! O my Mother Isle!
How shouldst thou prove aught else but dear and holy
To me, who from thy lakes and mountain-hills,
Thy clouds, thy quiet dales, thy rocks and seas,
Have drunk in all my intellectual life,
All sweet sensations, all ennobling thoughts,
All adoration of the God in nature,
All lovely and all honourable things,
Whatever makes this mortal spirit feel
Thy joy and greatness of its future being?

SAMUEL TAYLOR COLERIDGE

INTRODUCTION

The illustrations in this book show a bygone age. They recall an England of vast unspoiled spaces, when tourism was in its infancy and the lone walker could – without fear of rebuff or hostility – knock at the door of a strange cottage and ask for a glass of milk to refresh him after his exertions. His walk would be enlivened by the sight and sound of birds in their hundreds, and in the right season great sways of primroses and bluebells were a common sight along with the now so rare native orchids.

Edwardian travellers were not only indefatigable walkers, they were – like all educated men of the period – masters of many subjects. They had an informed interest in subjects ranging from literature to bird song and botany, from architectural history to the formation of the land.

Such a man was Roland Meredith, a widowed London schoolmaster of comfortable means who retired at the end of 1900 and spent his remaining years walking around England for the pleasure of visiting historical sites and admiring the countryside around them. The text of this book is taken from his diary for 1901, the year in which Queen Victoria died and a new era can be said to have begun. The pictures were all painted in the early 1900s by a variety of artists. The era they portray, prosperous and enjoyable as it was for the 'privileged classes', was a short one, for it ended abruptly in 1914 with the outbreak of the First World War. Meredith's journal and the illustrations that accompany it are therefore both a fascinating historical document and a nostalgic record of a lifestyle that was soon to be swept away.

Opposite

THE IDYLLIC VILLAGE OF HEADLEY, HAMPSHIRE

31 March 1901

I had planned to start my programme of walks earlier in the year, but the death of Her Majesty on 22 January cast such an air of mourning, old though she was, across the whole country that it seemed appropriate and respectful to wait. Strange that the ending of my old life and the beginning of what I hope will be a fruitful and enjoyable one should coincide so closely both with the start of a new century and with such a change in the mood and fortunes of our country with the accession of His Majesty, Edward VII.

I began my journeying at Farnham, one of the most westerly points in Surrey, for the simple reason that an easy train ride from London could bring me here to the heart of some pretty countryside and delightful rambles. From the station it is an easy stroll along the Hog's Back road to the well-wooded slopes of Crooksbury, which William Cobbett in his *Rural Rides* described as a mighty mountain, though it is to my mind little more than a steep incline. From the top there is an open look-out along the line of the Hog's Back to the north; in other directions the view is much impeded by the tall trees, ranked in sharp lines, that from some point suggest a gigantic yew clipped to a pattern.

An hour's walk by road through the foot of these woods would have brought me back to the meandering course of the river at Elstead, but at the cost of leaving out Tilford. I had been advised that I must turn off the path to the right and visit this picturesque village. I did so, and found it every bit as delightful as I had been led to hope, with its islanded green, its old bridges and the King's Oak,' a great tree reputed to have marked the boundary of the abbey lands in the reign of King Stephen, in the twelfth century.

Today was Sunday, so as my arrival at Tilford coincided with a late morning service, I thought fit to visit the church. As I came out a profusion of bird song fell upon my ears. I can never walk anywhere in southern England without thinking how beautifully its natural attractions are conveyed in the writings of W. H. Hudson; on this occasion I was reminded of his experience

A Lovely old Hump-backed Bridge near Elstead

of finding an isolated country church on just such a glorious spring day.

I was staying with the companion of my walks at a village in southern England in a district new to us. We arrived on a Saturday, and next morning after breakfast went out for a long walk. Turning into the first path across the fields on leaving the village, we came eventually to an oak wood, which was like an open forest, very wild and solitary. In half an hour's walk among the old oaks and underwood we saw no sign of human occupancy, and heard nothing but the woodland birds. We heard, and then saw, the cuckoo for the first time that season, though it was but April the fourth. But the cuckoo was early that spring and had been heard by some from the middle of March. At length, about half-past ten o'clock, we caught sight of a number of people walking in a kind of straggling procession by a path which crossed ours at right angles, headed by a stout old man in a black smock frock and brown leggings, who carried a big book in one hand. One of the processionists we spoke to told us they came from a hamlet a mile away on the borders of the wood and were on their way to church. We elected to follow them, thinking that the church was at some neighbouring village; to our surprise we found it was in the wood, with no other building in sight – a small ancient-looking church built on a raised mound, surrounded by a wide shallow grass-grown trench, on the border of a marshy stream. The people went in and took their seats, while we remained standing just by the door. Then the priest came from the vestry, and seizing the rope vigorously, pulled at it for five minutes, after which he showed us where to sit and the service began. It was very pleasant there, with the door open to the sunlit forest and the little green churchyard without, with a willow wren, the first I had heard, singing his delicate little strain at intervals.

Even some of the less common and less tame birds care as little for

The Heather in its Full Glory, Frensham Common

a man on a bicycle as they do for a cow. Not long ago a pewit trotted leisurely across the road not more than ten yards from my front wheel; and on the same day I came upon a green woodpecker enjoying a dust-bath in the public road. He declined to stir until I stopped to watch him, then merely flew about a dozen yards away and attached himself to the trunk of a fir tree at the roadside and waited there for me to go.

1 April

From Tilford beautiful rambles open alongside Frensham Ponds and out on to the heaths of Hindhead. On the other side of the river, fine commons rise up to the Hog's Back. Between these swelling and bristling heights, I followed the green valley of the Wey, which below Elstead again ties itself into knots of vagary, then beyond the Somerset Bridge begins to behave more prettily as it enters the park of Peperharow. To the left side stands Lord Midleton's mansion, near the church, restored from the designs of Pugin and enriched with interior ornamentation that make it one of the finest in this part of Surrey. The weather is wonderfully warm for the time of the year and the wild flowers are a joy to behold.

The Godalming high road, running by the south side of Peperharow, here deserts the Wey valley. Another road mounts up by the fine modern church of Shackleford and over the heights of Hurtmore. But the pedestrian should stay close to the left side of the Wey, passing under a high bank to the bend where, along a charming little bit of woodland, cleft by green gulleys, is reached a closed-in swimming place. Beyond this first sign of Godalming he gets on a road again, below that hillside suburb that has grown up about the transplanted Charterhouse School.

Pepys wrote the name of the place as 'Godliman'; and by old-fashioned folk in later days it was vernacularly spoken of as something like 'Gorlmin'. But with so scholastic a garrison in its citadel, Godalming is now in a position to define its spelling and pronunciation. The main part of the town lies out of

sight behind the other bank of the Wey, below which a trout of over 12lb was caught not many years ago; but coarse fish are the more frequent spoil of local anglers. Across the bridge the road took me by the church and up into the High Street, showing old inns, picturesque seventeenth-century dwellings and a quaint Market House near the upper end.

Godalming deserves to be admired as a good specimen of the English market-town. American visitors are always impressed that it is old enough to be mentioned in King Alfred's will. England has hundreds of such towns to show, but not many of them are surrounded by so beautiful a mingling of meadow and woodland, of hill, heath and water scenery. In all directions there are lovely walks and drives. The water tower over the Charterhouse shows the heights above the Wey, across which go roads to Loseley (at whose mansion Queen Elizabeth once stayed, causing great expense and anxiety to the then lord), Compton and the Hog's Back. On the opposite side a more distant tower rises upon a swell of woods, parks and heaths, through which is the way to Bramley and Wonersh.

Despite the temptations to follow any or all of these views, I kept to my path along the river, henceforth navigable by barges and restrained by locks. After a couple of miles a view of Guildford appeared in the gap in the Downs through which the Wey passes. On my right was the junction of the now-abandoned Wey and Arun Canal, its grass-grown trench making a peculiar but not unpleasing feature in the valley to the south-east, beneath the crests and clumps that hide Wonersh. The spire of Shalford Church welcomed me to another of the many so-called 'prettiest villages in Surrey', but I had another destination in sight and stuck to the towpath, which, except in wet weather, makes the best way forward, bordered as it is by noble trees hanging over from private grounds. And so, beside a picturesque mill-race, I reached the lower end of Guildford, near the railway station, where the playful river for the first time finds itself imprisoned by buildings.

Although Guildford is Surrey's county town, it is nowadays much

Sunset on the Water near Wonersh

overshadowed by Kingston and Croydon to the north, and I use it merely as a convenient place to rest for the night. Tomorrow the train will take me home to London, where I will spend the forthcoming Easter holiday. I do look forward to a few quiet days in my study and my old friend Geoffrey Hunter's visit. It will be nice to have news of the old school and to share my travelling impressions with him. Then I have a small northerly excursion and a long southern one planned before I venture again into another part of Surrey.

10 April

Hatfield in Hertfordshire is rightly renowned for the beauty of its Jacobean mansion, built by the first Earl of Salisbury, Robert Cecil, Secretary of State to Queen Elizabeth and largely responsible for assuring that on her death the crown passed to the Scottish king who became James I of England. Students of the period will know that it was in the Old Palace here that the young Princess Elizabeth spent much of her childhood; here that she was 'detained' during the reign of her sister Mary, and here that she learned of the latter's death and of her own succession to the throne.

But it was not Tudor history that drew me to Hertfordshire. Rather I had heard much of the beauties of the gardens of Brocket Hall, an eighteenth-century manor some three miles out of Hertfordshire, belonging now to Earl Cowper, and formerly the home of two Prime Ministers, Lord Melbourne and Lord Palmerston.

The house itself is unremarkable, but the setting is indeed picturesque, upon a slight hill in an attractive and well-wooded park, with the River Lea winding through. The formal ribbon gardens were full of gentle colour – delicate whites, blues, pinks and yellows – but I was told that in summer these gave way to riotous reds, oranges and scarlets. Not to everyone's taste, perhaps, but a tribute to the cheery nature of the plantsman who conceived them. I returned to London well contented with this excursion into botany.

Brocket Hall

24 April

I began my tour of Sussex in the little village of Bodiam, in the east of the county. This was partly so that I could spend a day or two with friends before setting out; partly because of its pleasant situation on the River Rother; and partly because the castle there, like so many on my Sussex itinerary, has much to attract the tourist with an interest in history.

Bodiam Castle was built in 1368, to deter the French from invading by means of the river. Most of us have been taught proudly that England has never been invaded since 1066, but during the Hundred Years War such an attack was a very real threat. Thanks to Henry II's marriage to Eleanor of Aquitaine some 200 years earlier, the English kings were dukes of that part of south-west France, but it had in the intervening period become a prosperous wine-producing region and thus a desirable property. This, coupled with the emerging nationalism of a French kingdom beginning for the first time to unite into the country we know today, lay at the heart of the Hundred Years War, and at the time Bodiam Castle was built the French, with their allies the Castilians, were carrying out a series of raids along the southern coast of England which resulted in great damage to the ports of Rye and Winchelsea. The castle is now a many-turreted shell, surrounded by a moat full of lilies, and a prettier location in Sussex would be hard to find.

27 April

A good day's stroll westward along the Rother brought me to Mayfield, a foothill of Ashdown Forest. In the morning the weather was unpromising but, as the day wore on, the sun came out and restored my spirits. This former royal hunting forest, once known as Lancaster Great Park, was granted by Edward III to his third son, John of Gaunt, Duke of Lancaster, in 1372. For almost three centuries, no one seems to have encroached on the Duchy of Lancaster's right to hunt deer here, but during the troubled years surrounding the Civil War animals were poached from the park, trees felled illegally and ore extracted to supply the local iron industry. Many of the

Bodiam Castle

massive oaks which had stood here since time immemorial were lost about this time, their timbers required to stoke the furnaces of their foundries. The Restoration of Charles II brought no end to the turbulence, for he leased the forest to the Earl of Dorset; the latter invited 'improvers' to enclose certain areas for the purposes of farming, to the annoyance of the local people who felt they had established the right to graze their livestock there. They retaliated by breaking down fences and trampling crops.

This conflict was resolved by statute in 1693, when over half the existing forest was permitted to be enclosed, leaving 6400 acres for common grazing. That area, with its magnificent views overlooking the Weald, forms what we now know as Ashdown Forest. As I gazed, I was reminded of a poem by James Thomson, which he called 'Britannia':

> Heavens! what a goodly prospect spreads around,
> Of hills, and dales, and woods, and lawns, and spires,
> And glittering towns, and gilded streams, till all
> The stretching landscape into smoke decays!
> Happy Britannia! where the Queen of Arts
> Inspiring vigour, liberty abroad
> Walks, unconfined, e'en to thy farthest cots,
> And scatters plenty with unsparing hand.
> Rich is thy soil, and merciful thy clime;
> Thy streams unfailing in the summer's drought;
> Unmatched thy guardian oaks.

Mayfield itself is a pretty village with remarkably preserved Tudor houses, the finest – that known as the Middle House – dating back to 1576, but it is for the views that I will remember this part of my journey.

29 April

On the north-eastern fringes of Ashdown Forest, on the very borders of Kent and Sussex, sits Groombridge, with its eighteenth-century tiled cottages

Mayfield

attractively arranged around a triangular green. The manor house here has been attributed to Wren; certainly it is of that period and both house and gardens are of an elegance to delight the eye.

While staying here I happened upon the work of a local writer who, attempting to define the county, wrote:

> Sussex was created from the sea. Its inhabitants and its invaders at all periods, save perhaps in the height of the Roman prosperity, and again during the last hundred and fifty years, have had a difficulty in going northward, because there spread north of the most habitable region the long belt of what is called the Weald. Sussex is, in a word, a great range of hills along the south coast inhabited upon either slope and upon either plain at either base, but cut off from the Thames Valley by a soil long uncultivated and more suited to forest than to habitation.

But this eastern portion of Sussex has long been exploited for its iron ore – possibly since pre-Roman times and certainly as recently as the Napoleonic Wars. Despite the unspoiled beauty of its countryside, therefore, it has never been as isolated as the words just quoted suggest. There is a lively, more industrious air about it than one finds in the west of the county. Two other historical and geographical features may be cited in further explanation of this – firstly, the proximity of Kent, with its great international highway leading from London to Dover; and secondly the early clearing of much of the forest, so that communication with the capital and the Thames Valley was established sooner and more easily than in the west.

Nowadays this part of the county is attracting a worrying number of newcomers who, having made their fortune in some large town or other, are seeking the 'old world' charm of these pretty little villages and despoiling them with great modern villas. Sadly, I fear it will not be long, particularly in the more accessible eastern part, before the 'South Countryness' that has

Garden of the Moated House, Groombridge

Garden of the Moated House, Groombridge   Wilfrid Ball 1904

25

given Sussex its identity for so many centuries is lost in suburban sprawl.

1 May

East Grinstead, which I reached by following the Kent/Sussex border to the west for a day, does not cause me such pain, for it has always – for 700 years at least – been a busy market town; now it is merely busier than before. Its charter dates from 1221, and outside the town stands a magnificent Jacobean house, Sackville College, founded by the Earl of Dorset as a home for the poor and disabled. I seem to have been unlucky with my choice of hostelry over the last three nights. The first one was terribly noisy while the second had such lumpy beds as so make sleep equally impossible.

6 May

Pulborough is situated where the waters of the River Rother meet those of the River Arun, in the shadow of the South Downs. The foundations of the town are almost certainly Roman, and the position was a strategic one in those times, for it was here that the great Roman road linking Chichester on the south coast to London crossed the Arun.

The first fifty miles of this road, known as Stane Street, can still be traced on a large-scale map. From the east gate of Chichester to the point where it passes close to the race-course at Epsom, there are only small and largely explicable gaps. The Romans, as is well known, built their roads as straight as the lie of the country allowed, and with one exception (where the line must have been diverted because of unsuitable ground and the road is lost in fields) it heads straight from Chichester to the Downs, where it follows a high ridge for several miles. On the open grass of the Downs it still marks the boundary between fields, where once it must have differentiated one property from another. Descending the north side of the Downs a deviation is rememberedin the name of the farm – Cold Harbour – a common name on English maps

Opposite:

East Grinstead in 1904

26

High St. East Grinstead
Wilfrid Ball 1904.

which derives from the Latin *curbare*, to curve, and marks a point where the topography interfered with the Romans' love of straight lines.

At the bottom of the hill lies Bignor, a tiny village which boasts the best preserved Roman pavement in England. Between Bignor and Pulborough the route cannot be divined with any certainty, especially in the last mile or so, which is ancient marshland, once crossed by a causeway. In a period such as that following the Roman departure from Britain, when maintenance of roads and causeways was entirely neglected, such a path would inevitably have disappeared into the soft soil below. But if one lays a ruler on an Ordnance map between Bignor and the next hard piece of road beyond Pulborough, the straight line it follows crosses literally within a yard or two of the existing Pulborough Bridge. It is therefore hard to resist the exciting conclusion that this is the very route followed by the Roman legions.

There is mention of Pulborough in the Domesday Book, as there is of a surprising number of settlements on the south coast and villages along the Arun, showing how developed this area was at the end of the eleventh century. The origins of Pulborough church, with its delightful lych gate and twelfth-century frescoes, are known to be Norman.

8 May

Midhurst, being that much further from the sea, is of later date. It is first recorded as being a borough as late as the fourteenth century, in the reign of Edward II. But it must have become a prosperous market town shortly thereafter, for it boasts several fine medieval inns. An old tradition persists from this time in the nightly ringing of 'curfew' at the parish church. It is said that a rider lost in the darkness found his way to Midhurst by following the sound of the church bells; in gratitude he bought a piece of land, still called Curfew Gardens, in the town and presented it to the citizens of Midhurst on condition that the bell be rung every night.

Pulborough

At Midhurst I found myself once more on the Rother, with glorious scenery all around and yet more beautiful villages to every side. In one of them, South Harting, I came upon a delightful thatched cottage of the kind much favoured by watercolour artists and, on enquiry, found more interest than I would have expected in the manner of their construction:

Local materials having much to do with the structure, the type of dwelling that we may expect to find in counties where wood was plentiful, and the cost of preparing and putting it on the ground less than that of quarrying, shaping, and carrying stone, is the picturesque, timber-formed cottage.

The construction is simple in the extreme. A plan was set out and a base or foundation wall built, usually of brick or stone, high enough to keep the sill well above the ground. Into this sill heavy posts of timber, some eight or nine inches square, were fixed upright, about seven or eight feet apart. Upon these main posts beams were laid across the building, projecting forward some eighteen inches in front of the framing, and showing in the rooms below. Into the beams others were connected longitudinally, and to these latter again the floor joists were tenoned, projecting the same distance as the main beams. The framing of the upper storey then followed that of the ground floor, the sill being now laid on the ends of the overhanging timbers.

The roof-tree was always of hand-hewn oak, and it was this which gave many of the old roofs their pleasant curves away from the central chimney. The unseasoned sawn deal of the modern roof may sway in any direction.

In the older houses the rooms were low and the roof was carried down well over the side walls, so that the upper storey was usually badly lighted and worse ventilated. Little use was made

The Old Mill Pool, Midhurst

of the large space in the roof, but this omission adds much to the picturesqueness of the exterior, for the roofs gain in simplicity by their unbroken surface and treatment. It is somewhat surprising that the old builders did not recognise this costly disregard of space.

The roofs, like the framework, testified to the geological formation and agricultural conditions of the district. In those where the land was chiefly arable, or the distance from market considerable, wheaten thatch was the usual and most comfortable covering, for it is warm in winter and cool in summer, just the reverse of the tiles or slates which have practically supplanted it.

12 May

Chichester is the principal town of the belt of West Sussex which lies between the Downs and the sea. Its origins predate the Roman invasion, for it was the capital of the country inhabited by an ancient tribe called the Regni. Little else is known of the history of Sussex in this time, nor indeed of the 400 years of Roman occupation – except that, as we have seen, the Romans left far more physical evidence of their presence and of the prosperous civilisation which they brought to this island than they did documents which might have answered the many questions about them which have puzzled later generations.

The Romans called the town on this site Noviomagus and when, in Saxon times, it had fallen into ruin, the local chieftain, Aella, gave it to his son Cissa, who named it after himself – Cissa's Castle or *Ceaster*. The chief feature of interest nowadays is the Norman cathedral, whose tapering 277-foot spire can be seen across the coastal plain for miles around. From Norman times throughout the Middle Ages it was the church rather than any military or civil authority that ruled the town and its surrounds.

The reason for this is closely tied up with the geography of the country. For

South Harting

administrative purposes the efficient Normans divided Sussex into six regions known as rapes, running approximately north/south, so that each was bounded to the south by the sea. Of these the Rape of Chichester is the westernmost. To the west of it lie marshes; to the north and east it is bounded by the Downs and by what was for many years inhospitable, inarable sandy ground – an empty desert producing no corn, incapable of supporting the needs of an invading or occupying army. So although the harbour is large and shallow, affording an easy entry to England in the early days, once past the town there was nowhere satisfactory for an invader to go. Such an invader would have been better advised to make his landing point further east and (in the days before such fortresses as Bodiam) advance along the Rother or the Arun.

Thus topography explains why there has never been an important castle nor a major battle in the Rape of Chichester (though the suffix to its name suggests that it was fortified in Roman or Saxon times). This fact goes some way to explaining the peculiar dominance of the church here. But on the other hand the rape's freedom from military intervention was also partially due to respect for the power the church *already* held. It is easy for us in our scientific age to forget what an important part the church played in men's lives for a thousand years after the fall of the Roman Empire, and of the distinction there was between civil and ecclesiastical rule. As one writer puts it:

> We see it in a thousand ways illuminating the history of the Middle Ages; by way of sanctuary, by way of the ecclesiastical courts, by way of the atonement which men paid for violence when they founded great monasteries, by way of the technical abstention from capital sentences which the Church rigorously preserved.

Opposite:

Chichester Cross

34

Chichester Cross
Wilfrid Ball 1904

These are all ways in which the laws of the church stood apart from those of the rest of the land. In this context, it is interesting to observe that the parish of Slindon was included in the Rape of Chichester, although it should more logically have fallen into that of Arundel. But Slindon, although geographically in Sussex, was part of the property belonging to the see of Canterbury, and it may be that its powerful ecclesiastical owners preferred it to be administered by the pacific men of Chichester rather than those of the fortified and potentially war-mongering Rape of Arundel. As a footnote to this observation, Stephen Langton, controversial Archbishop of Canterbury in the early years of the thirteenth century, whose signature heads the list of witnesses to Magna Carta, died in Slindon in 1228.

13 May

I could not leave the region of Chichester without repairing to Bosham, that quaintly situated village on a peninsula between two tidal creeks, whose only road is frequently inundated at high water. It is from here that Canute is said to have ordered the tide to retreat. Sadly the history books make no serious mention of this whimsical incident. Canute is recorded as a ruthless conqueror who turned himself into a civilised law-giver and founded many monasteries. But having been King of England for three years, he inherited his native kingdom of Denmark on the death of his brother. To enable the country to function during his ensuing long absences, Canute undid much of the good he had done by dividing England into four powerful earldoms – Wessex, Mercia, Northumbria and East Anglia – and paving the way for further power struggles among his nobles. I was interested to read that one of the nobles thus created was Leofric of Mercia, who was married to Lady Godiva – I was to discover more about them when my travels took me north to Coventry.

Opposite:

St Richard's Walk, Chichester

It is also from Bosham that Harold of Wessex set sail in 1064 or 1065 to visit Duke William of Normandy and, according to Norman chronicles, to swear that William should be offered the crown of England on the death of Edward the Confessor. Other versions of the story suggest that Harold fell into William's hands by misadventure and was forced to swear the oath. This is the version suggested by the Bayeux Tapestry, which perhaps lends credence to the opinion, held by some, that the tapestry was worked not by Norman but by Saxon hands. The tapestry also shows Harold taking mass at Bosham Church before embarking on this ill-fated voyage.

14 May

The situation of Arundel is one of the most spectacular of all the river towns of England. To north and south the Arun flows through uninspiring country. From Pulborough it runs almost due south across marshes and then traverses the woods of Arundel Park, until it reaches the base of the hill on which the town is built. Below Arundel it becomes tidal, running in a deep channel with salt meadows on either side, until it enters the sea at Littlehampton, seven miles away. But Arundel stands on a steep bank, looking down on the river and towards the sea, dominated by its castle, but with all its other visible architecture entirely in keeping with its site.

The castle was built by Robert Montgomery, Earl of Shrewsbury, shortly after the conquest, to defend the valley against invasion from the sea. It was extended twice in the twelfth century, almost destroyed by a badly aimed cannonball in Cromwell's time, rebuilt in the eighteenth century and extensively restored in the last years of the nineteenth. The recent work was carried out using local flint from the Downs, and is a fine example of the technique of flint-dressing – the cutting of the outer surface of the stone. As it was explained to me:

> The separate dressing of so many small stones is an expensive matter, and it is probably the very expense which is so incurred, or rather the great expenditure of energy connoted by the appearance

BOSHAM

of such work, which impresses and is designed to impress the spectator of it.

Certainly those who love this Sussex tradition will be content to notice how well it has been preserved at Arundel.

There are no Roman relics in Arundel, although the town is thought to be as old as Chichester and all but the most pedantic historians believe that there was at the least a river crossing here in Roman times. Certainly there has been a town here for as long as there has been a fortress, and it seems likely that it very quickly became a substantial settlement, not much different in size from the modern town. It probably held a market for centuries before it was actually licensed to do so – many towns did – and it would certainly have offered such services to the garrison as butchers, money-changers, barbers (for Englishmen of the Middle Ages were generally clean-shaven) and carriers of every description. There is a story, sadly unsupported by anything more powerful than conjecture, that the fortress was linked by an underground passage to Amberley Castle, some seven miles to the north, which now lies in ruins. This fortress, like Arundel Castle, occupied a prime military position in the landscape of Sussex. Amberley was quite unattainable from the north and the west as it lay among dangerous marshes which were drained in later years. From the east the approach was also difficult. Only from the south was there a narrow gap on the brow of the Downs as they descended towards the river Arun.

It is thought that the bridge at Arundel is Roman in its origin, although is cannot be proven. It used to cross the river further downstream. The modern Arundel High Street was originally directly in line to the old bridge. It is thought that the Bridge Hotel was built exactly between the ancient and the present bridges.

20 May

Lewes has probably had strategic importance since pre-Roman times, but

Arundel Castle - Early Evening

reliable documentary evidence begins only towards the end of the Saxon period. In the reign of Athelstan (925–939), four mints were permitted to be established in Sussex, of which two were in Lewes (the others were at Chichester and Hastings), suggesting that it was at the time the most important settlement in the whole county. Like Chichester and Arundel, it was the centre of one of the six rapes established by the Normans.

The castle, largely Norman but built on the remains of a Saxon fortification, is little more than a ruin now, but it was once the home of William of Warren, son-in-law of the Conqueror; he was the first ruler of the Rape of Lewes and would have been effectively head of the garrison, responsible for guarding the peace of the county, and overlord of the many villages and manors in the surrounding area, from which he collected taxes. The honour attaching to this office must have been a reward for the younger William's services at the Battle of Hastings, where he is said to have fought with valour.

The student of history in Lewes may further revel in the warren of medieval streets and inns, or seek out Southover, one of several houses given by Henry VIII to Anne of Cleves in compensation after their divorce.

21 May

From Lewes I returned to the coast and to the part of the south coast which inspires me with most awe – Beachy Head. Towering some 534 feet above the sea, it affords on a clear day a view that stretches from the Isle of Wight in the west to Dungeness in the east. The chalky whiteness of the cliffs here rivals anything to be seen near Dover, and the fulmars that flit in and out of chinks in the rocks fill the air with their cries.

I thought of Tennyson, who admired the sight and sounds of the English Channel as I do:

Opposite:

Lewes Castle

You came, and looked, and loved the view
Long-known and loved by me,
Green Sussex fading into blue
With one gray glimpse of sea.

And Matthew Arnold, although he was thinking of Dover, could have been here in Sussex when he wrote:

The sea is calm to-night.
The tide is full, the moon lies fair
Upon the straits – on the French coast the light
Gleams and is gone; the cliffs of England stand
Glimmering and vast, out in the tranquil bay.
Come to the window, sweet is the night-air!
Only, from the long line of spray
Where the sea meets the moon-blanched land,
Listen! you hear the grating roar
Of pebbles which the waves draw back and fling,
At their return, up the high strand,
Begin and cease, and then again begin,
With tremulous cadence slow, and bring
The eternal note of sadness in.

24 May

The Romans built Pevensey Castle on the sea shore, as a defence against barbarian invaders. It was a mighty fortress, covering ten acres, and in the third century the Roman legions could bring their long boats right up to its gate. Since then the sea has retreated and left the castle – rebuilt by the

Opposite:

BEACHY HEAD

Normans using the Romans' material but in ruins now – two miles inland. Even as a ruin it is vast and dwarfs the village around it.

The very name of Pevensey suggests that the place is ancient. It is of Celtic origin and probably means 'the fortification at the far end of the wood'. This would have been an accurate description of Pevensey's status and situation – the Roman town on the same spot was called Anderida, derived from the Celtic forest of Andred, which covered the Weald and which the Saxons later called the Andreswald. In those days the lands to north and east of the castle were marshy flats in a shallow bay, covered over at high tide and forming a harbour protected on every side except the north-east. That harbour was probably deepened in Roman times and is known to have been used by the Normans, for it was here that William the Conqueror landed on his way to invade England.

With a brisk south-westerly wind behind him, William could have made the crossing from Normandy to Sussex in daylight on almost any day of the year, except perhaps midwinter. Certainly, despite delays due to bad weather, there was light enough for him on that day at the end of September 1066 when he arrived to claim the crown of England from Harold of Wessex.

Harold – that same Harold who had sworn , though perhaps under duress, to ensure that William became King of England – had, on the death of Edward the Confessor in January of 1066, accepted the crown himself. And the Duke of Normandy was not his only rival. During the summer, Harold Hardrada of Norway – who, having inherited part of Canute's empire, thought to lay claim to the rest of it – had invaded Northumbria and occupied York. Harold of Wessex, expecting an attack from Normandy, had prepared an army in the south and was compelled to march hastily northward. On 25 September Harold Hardrada was defeated and killed by Harold's forces at the Battle of Stamford Bridge. A mere three days later William landed at Pevensey.

PEVENSEY CASTLE

The rest of the story is well known. Harold's forces, exhausted and now ill-prepared, made haste to return south and encamped on a hill near the place we now call Battle. William met him there on 14 October. In a battle that lasted all day, the English position – on the crest of a hill and surrounded by a wall of shields – at first seemed impregnable, but sections of Harold's army were encouraged to break away from the core by real or feigned retreats on the part of the Normans. These smaller groups of Englishmen were quickly surrounded and overwhelmed, and the Normans were assured of victory well before dusk, when Harold received that fatal blow from the arrow.

Historians argue about the exact site of the Battle of Hastings, but it seems reasonable to suppose that it is where tradition sites it: on a rounded hill above the valley of the Brede, known as Hastings Plain. If it seems odd to an outsider that even such a small hill should be referred to as a plain, it is not so in Sussex, where many uplands are given the name of a neighbouring, settled part of the lowlands, possibly because the upland in question formed part of the same estate.

William founded Battle Abbey – dedicated to St Martin – having sworn an oath that he would do so should he win the battle. According to tradition the high altar marks the very spot where Harold fell. Throughout the Middle Ages Battle was the richest abbey in the area: at the time of the Dissolution of the Monasteries, the abbot surrendered to Henry VIII revenues of £1000 a year – a vast sum. The neighbouring abbey of Boxgrove recorded only £150.

Battle has never functioned as an abbey since those times, but among the surviving buildings are a fine fourteenth-century gatehouse.

The weather has been cold and windy for the last few days and I must admit that I am beginning to look forward to a few days at home in early June. Nevertheless, I am enjoying every hour of this journey and I often think how I used to long for the freedom to travel while I was still teaching.

BATTLE ABBEY

30 May

The last point on my tour of Sussex brings me back again almost to Kent. Although Rye is not mentioned in the Domesday Book, we know it to have been in existence at that time. It sits at the mouth of the Rother and was an important seaport in the Middle Ages, but entry to its harbour is difficult and, as a port, Rye has long been in decline. A local chronicle explained it thus:

> It is an almost universal rule that old harbours from which the sea has retreated, but to which the waterway still exists, are difficult of access, and Rye is no exception to this rule. There extends for more than a mile from the shore a mass of peaty mud through which the sea-bed of the river winds in a most tortuous fashion; at half-tide it is almost impossible to follow it if one has had no local experience. The matter is made worse from the fact that the channel is very poorly marked; its first entrance from the sea is impossible to discover in thick weather and not too easy upon a clear day. All this is a pity, for if Rye were still as accessible as is say Arundel, or even Bosham, it would form the most charming of all entries into the country, with its pyramid of old red roofs and its deep and visible history.

I recently read of the fears expressed by another writer: 'Unless there should arise some local industry which will make it worth while to dredge the river and establish an expensive system of leading marks into its mouth,' he wrote, 'Rye within another hundred years will be no more than Sandwich.'

I am no sailor and for me Rye is a delightfully quaint place with its cobbled streets and its centuries-old roofs which have resisted the combined onslaughts of wind and rain. I reached the town on a particularly wild day and never was I more pleased to see the pyramid of red roofs belonging to the Mermaid Inn, which opened 1420 and stands on a steep cobbled street which cannot have changed much from that day to this. I repaired there for

RYE, FROM CAMBER

51

afternoon tea and it was a delight to stretch my weary limbs in front of the fire which had been lit in recognition of the unseasonable weather. Lashings of hot tea and a plateful of delicious toasted tea-cakes soon cheered me up.

6 June

After a couple of days at home and a short visit to my dear late wife's sister and brother-in-law, I felt fully restored in body and spirit and ready for my next venture which would take me to northern Surrey, an area I had neglected on my previous visit. The views over the Holmesdale valley were among some of the best I have seen in the country. Here the River Mole turns towards Box Hill, once known as White Hill. Sadly it has been somewhat denuded of box trees since the days when it made a favourite excursion for visitors to Epsom Spa or when Jane Austen's Emma so offended poor Miss Bates with her unthinking wit. But it is a grandly wooded face under which the river crosses the Holmesdale valley, on the other side winding round the avenues of Betchworth Park, where stand the so-called castle ruins that are really those of a tumble-down mansion. Above the park the Mole passes the trim village green of Brockham then, opposite a huge chalk scar on the Downs, winds up the valley to Betchworth Church.

One might now expect the Mole to run down the Holmesdale valley, between the chalk and the sandstone; but this river seems seldom to do what might be expected of it. Over a dip in the sand heights it comes from the south, draining the wet Wealden clays beyond, where it is fed by more tributaries than there are forks of the Missouri. The main stream passes by Horley and between the two arms of the Brighton road. But all the peaceful expanse of meadows, fields and woods stretching westward to the Horsham road is seamed by its branching brooks, one of the largest of which is called the Deanoaks, a name recalling the fame of this soil for these great trees.

Among the vagaries of these modest streams, roads almost as crooked, or reaches of green path, would have taken me to any number of secluded villages lying within a square of a few miles – chief among them Leigh (the

way to which must be asked for as *Lie*), which is commonly sought out for its church brasses and for the weathered mansions now reduced to farmhouses, one of them according to tradition a haunt of Ben Jonson; and Charlwood, with its fine old church, distinguished by a noble screen and decayed frescoes. Capel has less to recommend it, except for the adjacent station of Ockley, from which, under the face of Leith Hill, the visitor may gain access to more popular scenes. All this edge of the county makes a pleasant rambling ground, with many picturesque spots that tend to lie outside the scope of guide books.

On the south side of Leith Hill, showing such a bold face to the flats of Ockley, the line of the Roman Road coincides with the modern one – still known as 'Stone Street causeway' – which was ascribed by country folk in the seventeenth century to the work of the Devil.

Ockley itself is one of the pleasantest of Surrey villages (there are so many of them!), clustered about a broad green, beside which Stone Street has grown into a lordly avenue, shadowing what seems a Roman-like massiveness of paving. Around it, though still within the bounds of Surrey, green byways wind among swelling ridges and clumps of timber thick-set on the edge of the Weald. To the north rises the stiff ascent of Leith Hill, which I decided to keep for the following day.

7 June

Leith Hill is the highest point not only of Surrey, but also in this corner of England. The topmost knoll on its southern brow stands 965 feet above the sea and is crowned by a tower that adds nearly a hundred feet to the natural elevation. The tower was built in the eighteenth century by a local squire

Opposite:

Betchworth Church

named Hull, apparently a 'character', who had himself buried in it, to the scandal of his neighbours.

It is only on the southern side that Leith Hill makes a clear show of its height. The northern slopes are gentle, falling gradually for three or four miles into the Holmesdale valley. The broken contours of the sand are richly clad with woods, parks, commons, heather and bracken; they are patched too with quagmires and ragged gravel pits, and seamed with lanes and hedgerows, so that all the most shaggily picturesque features of Surrey are here mixed together, in contrast with the smoother and barer outlines of the chalk Downs, like a mastiff lying side by side with a collie.

Standing on the craggy knoll, one has at last a clear view to the south, and from the top of the tower can overlook, it is said, thirteen counties, spread out all round as on a map, shaded and dotted and streaked with heights, woods, streams, villages, churches and farms, melting away or running together in the distance like the smoke from a myriad of English homes. In the foreground lie the leafy lowlands of the Weald, bounded by the line of the South Downs, through a gap in which the sea might come into view, weather permitting. The well-travelled John Evelyn calls this the best prospect he ever beheld; and if he may be suspected of local prejudice, having been born near Dorking, a later commentator, the critic and playwright John Dennis, best remembered today as the victim of the satire of Pope and Swift, is found breaking out into enthusiasm over a scene which he declares to surpass the finest in Italy.

Here one ought to produce a poetical description; but, so far as I know, the bards who must have often looked from Leith Hill seem to have been struck dumb by admiration.

Opposite:

SPRING EVENING IN THE WOODS NEAR OCKLEY

8 June

Some question exists as to the precise route of that part of the Pilgrims' Way along which my travels took me today. This is a prehistoric track along the North Downs which the faithful followed to the tomb of Thomas à Becket at Canterbury and which, had they chosen to direct their steps in the opposite direction, would have led them all the way to Winchester. At a certain point the original road would naturally have turned up to Shalford, the shallow ford, whose church spire, village stocks and picturesque old mill invite wayfarers to a slight diversion. But the convenience of a ferry almost opposite St Catherine's Chapel must have straightened out the pilgrims' track.

From this point it runs on over a park sward, then across the high road up to an avenue under whose shade path, lane and overgrown roadway go side by side. After falling into the path over the Downs from Guildford, and crossing a sandy descending lane, there is marked on the left a 'bridle road to Albury', which leads straight up by St. Martha's Chapel. This chapel, a prominent landmark on a 500-foot swell of heath and copse, seems to have had its name corrupted from 'Martyrs' Hill', perhaps from *Sancti Martyris*, and to be really a shrine of St Thomas, which would claim the special devotion that pilgrims to Canterbury have shown for this spot.

At Tyting Farm below is an oratory of the twelfth or thirteenth century, taken to have been the residence of the priest in charge. The chapel itself, after long standing in ruins, was restored in the middle of the nineteenth century, and Sunday services are held here. The weekday pilgrim will halt to enjoy the prospect of the Tillingbourne valley before him, edged to his left by the Downs, which a little way farther on have their famous viewpoint at Newlands Corner, said to be named from Abraham Newland,

Opposite:

OLD SURREY FARM

described as 'the most popular author of England' in his time, as it was his signature that validated the notes issued by the Bank of England, then made at Chilworth in the valley below St Martha's. The bank-note factory has gone, but still here stand the gunpowder mills; and here too was once a well-known printing establishment, now ruined by fire. On the south side of St Martha's the view ranges over a hollow filled with commons, woods and miniature lakes.

Here the conscientious guide should hesitate over how best to advise the seeker after the picturesque to progress. For in this part of Surrey the rambler finds himself among an embarrassment of scenic riches. There is hardly such another walk in England as that dozen miles or so along the top of the Downs between Guildford and Dorking. From St Martha's Hill I ascended to the stretch named the Roughs, a beautiful wilderness of beeches, yews, thorns, holly and other chalk-loving copse-wood tangled in bracken and bramble. On the further side of this ridge there is a straight way up from Clandon Station, coming out at Newlands Corner. As to the rutted grassy track along the Downs, its merit lies in its romantic loneliness: hardly a house comes into view between Newlands Corner and Ranmore Common, where the crash of a woodman's axe may recall American backwoods.

The pilgrims of old days seldom took more trouble than they could help, and their way lay below, near the foot of the Downs, where, after Chilworth, Albury is the next village. One notable resident was Martin Tupper, that once widely read proverbial philosopher whose name became a source of mirth for a later generation when to sneer at it became a commonplace with every petty critic. For my part, I think the man who could write 'A good book is the best of friends, the same to-day and for ever' shows, if not great originality, then at least sound common sense.

But Mr Tupper was untroubled by the wind of criticism; for in his case it was tempered by the most robust self-applause. His literary memoirs are vertiable torrents of prose and verse flowing from a truly fountain pen. Mr Tupper

was, among other things, the high priest of Albury's 'Silent Pool', as he christened that stretch of water known to the locals as Sherbourne Pond. The pool is said to be haunted by the spirit of a bathing maiden on whom King John spied as Actaeon did on Diana; but, unlike the myth, it was not the intruder who came by his deserts, but rather the modest damsel who drowned in her fright.

This deep chalk basin of crystal water prettily set in a wooded dell is now one of the great attractions of the area, yet so secluded that many seekers pass it by unseen. It has been lately stated in the newspapers that the Silent Pool was being sucked dry by waterworks on the Downs; but since then I have found it deep and clear and cool as ever. Can it be that what we read in newspapers is not always true?

13 June

My last stop in Surrey was at that wide stretch of the Surrey Commons which almost covers the county's western edge and extends into Berkshire. Defoe speaks of the bed of 'Bagshot sands' lying between the Hog's Back and the Thames valley as a dismal desert, over which indeed the traveller was once fain to hasten, keeping a sharp look-out for Bedouins in breeches. But the Sahara itself is not everywhere so black as it has been painted, and this Surrey wilderness has many an oasis of park and farm, gardened villages such as Chobham, pine-crested knolls and tangled dells, all the greener in contrast with their environment of dry slopes.

Chobham (not to be confused with Cobham in the Mole valley, nor with the Kentish Cobham mentioned in *The Pickwick Papers*) was the camp for military training and exercise in the summer before the Crimean War. About an hour's walk from Woking Junction, it is still so far out of the way as to

Opposite:

SILENT POOL

remain an old-world Surrey village straggling round its ancient church. The camp was mainly on its north-eastern skirts, and was pitched for only two or three months. Controversy with influential residents is said to have stood in the way of the village being permanently occupied by Bellona, the Roman goddess of war always apt to be considered a demoralising companion to the rustic Venus; but although the troops are now removed to Aldershot, the village has a Russian cannon to show as a souvenir of its flirtation with the War Office.

From Chobham I returned to London, whence the next part of my journey would take me westward into Hampshire.

25 June

I have always much admired W. H. Hudson's description of a view over Hampshire and envied him a comical experience he had in a village there:

> From Newbury and the green meadows of the Kennet the Hampshire hills may be seen, looking like the South Down range at its highest point viewed from the Sussex Weald. I made for Coombe Hill, the highest hill in Hampshire, and found it a considerable labour to push my machine up from the pretty tree-hidden village of East Woodhay at its foot. The top is a league-long tableland, with stretches of green elastic turf, thickets of furze and bramble, and clumps of ancient noble beeches – a beautiful lonely wilderness with rabbits and birds for only inhabitants. From the highest point where a famous gibbet stands for ever a thousand feet above the sea and where there is a dew-pond, the highest in England, which has never dried up although a large flock of sheep drink in it every summer day, one looks down into an immense hollow, a Devil's Punch Bowl very many times magnified, and spies, far away and far below, a few lonely houses half hidden by trees at the bottom. This is the romantic village of Coombe, and

THE BOURNE, CHOBHAM

thither I went and found the vicar busy in the garden of the small old picturesque parsonage.

Here a very pretty little bird comedy was in progress: a pair of stock-doves which had been taken from a rabbit-hole in the hill and reared by hand had just escaped from the large cage where they had always lived, and all the family were excitedly engaged in trying to recapture them. They were delightful to see – those two pretty blue birds with red legs running busily about on the green lawn, eagerly searching for something to eat and finding nothing. They were quite tame and willing to be fed, so that anyone could approach them and put as much salt on their tails as he liked, but they refused to be touched or taken; they were too happy in their new freedom, running and flying about in that brilliant sunshine, and when I left towards the evening they were still at large.

My own travels in Hampshire began not so very far from this scene, on the River Itchen, at a point north-east of Winchester on which many pretty villages stand. All the villages on this stretch of the river are pretty in an old-world way, with their ancient churches and thatched cottages. Their Saxon names are as picturesque as their locations and remind us that it was the Saxon who broke this land to the plough, settling along the river valleys where his Celtic predecessor had chosen to remain on higher ground. In the space of about eight miles I wandered past Ovington, Itchen Stoke, Itchen Abbas, Martyr Worthy, Easton, Headbourne Worthy, King's Worthy, Abbot's Worthy – Saxon in origin every one of them.

Perhaps the prettiest of all is Itchen Abbas. Here I paused for refreshment at the Plough Inn, where Charles Kingsley wrote part of *The Water Babies* some forty years ago, and stood for a while on the charming bridge below the mill to watch the great trout in the water beneath, after some of whose ancestors Kingsley doubtless angled, keen sportsman that he was. And I admired the giant yew tree in the churchyard, under which the faithful of

FORTON, NEAR LONGPARISH

Itchen Abbas were buried for centuries before either Kingsley or I were thought of.

Or perhaps – because with such abundance of beauty it is difficult finally to prefer one place over another – the prettiest of all is Easton, which seems to belong to another world. The river is clear and sparkling, the trout large and tempting, the coots and moorhens elusive and endearing. The variety of style of the thatched roofs is equalled only by the range of shapes and sizes into which the yew trees are clipped. The Norman porch of the church is remarkably well preserved and must attract any student of the architecture of the period.

But Headbourne Worthy boasts an even older church, possibly the oldest in Hampshire. Certainly its origins are Saxon. Here is to be found an ancient relic that, despite being much defaced, cannot fail to be of interest – a Saxon stone crucifix which once adorned the outside of the west wall, but is now sheltered by a later addition to the fabric of the church. The yews at Kings Worthy are clipped into square shapes, to match the squareness of the church tower.

26 June

If the outskirts of Winchester are pleasing, the city is, of course, magnificent, as befits the place that was the capital of England for many centuries in Saxon and Norman times. Approaching it alone, I remembered the words of William Hazlitt written after a country walk:

> How fine it is to enter some old town, walled and turreted, just at the approach of night-fall, or to come to some straggling village, with the lights streaming through the surrounding gloom; and then

Opposite:

Itchen Abbas

after enquiring for the best entertainment the place affords, to 'take one's ease at one's inn!' These eventful moments in our lives are in fact too precious, too full of solid, heart-felt happiness to be frittered and dribbled away in imperfect sympathy. I would have them all to myself, and drain them to the last drop: they will do to talk of or to write about afterwards.

So I spent a solitary evening in a charming inn within sight of Winchester Cathedral, which I planned to explore the next day.

27 June

Winchester was an important town in Saxon times, but the Norman – I will not say conquest, for here it was surely a deluge – swept all that away and left its own indelible marks. Of these, first and foremost is the cathedral. Here in the northern and southern transepts the Norman masonry seems hardly to have been touched in a thousand years, although the fabric of the rest of the building has been much altered and extended. One of those additions, the retro-choir to the east, dates from the reign of Richard I and was built on such inadequate foundations that extensive and expensive repairs are being carried out to this day.

Of the many features of interest, I felt most inclined to linger over the chapel dedicated to William of Waynflete, a remarkable educationalist of the fifteenth century who was headmaster of Winchester College, then chosen by Henry VI to become the first headmaster of his new school at Eton. From this position he rose to be Provost of Eton , Bishop of Winchester and finally Lord Chancellor of England. He played a part in suppressing Jack Cade's rebellion, was an important adviser to his king and in the course of a very long life also had time to found Magdalen College, Oxford.

Opposite:

MARTYR WORTHY

Architecturally, the altar screen is perhaps the greatest gem in the cathedral, a perfect example of Perpendicular Gothic, rich and varied in detail without being florid, and exquisitely executed. The many memorials to those buried within the cathedral include almost all the Bishops of Winchester, notably the canonised Swithin, who is said originally to have been buried *outside* the cathedral. According to tradition, the monks of the tenth century, some hundred years after Swithin's death, wished to exhume his body and bury it within the newly rebuilt cathedral. Presumably the late bishop objected to this profanity, for on the appointed day (15 July) it rained violently and the ceremony was perforce delayed. Hence arose the tradition that if it rains on St Swithin's Day, which is still celebrated on 15 July, it will rain every day for forty days.

Among the many other great names inextricably associated with Winchester one cannot forget William of Wykeham – like Waynflete a combination of churchman, politician and educationalist. Bishop of Winchester in 1367, he was twice Chancellor of England, under Edward III and Richard II, and founded Winchester School in 1382.

Although there had been schools in England before, Wykeham's 'New Sainte Marie College of Wynchester' can with justification be described as the mother of English public schools. Earlier educational establishments such as the King's School at Canterbury had been appendages to and dependent on religious institutions. Wykeham's school was an independent, self-governing body, with much of the discipline carried out by the boys themselves. And although in recent years there have grown up many detractors of this system, Wykeham certainly intended it to lay the foundation not only of intellectual excellence but of excellence in personal qualities too. The original meaning of the school motto 'Manners Makyth Man' is more clearly understood if one recognises that 'manners' is a translation of the Latin *mores*, and perhaps better rendered as 'character'.

One enters the college through the ancient Outer Gate and sees the image of

'Sainte Marie' over the Middle Gate – scholars, as the pupils of the school are still called, doff their hats as a gesture of respect to the Virgin whenever they cross the courtyard. Across the Chantry Court ones finds the Chapel and the Great Hall, the Chapel cloisters being perhaps the most spiritual part of the whole school, where one is tempted simply to wander and dream of the past; the Hall being one of the grandest of its kind it has been my privilege to visit. Approached up an imposing stairway, it has a magnificent old timber roof and carved wainscotting.

The history of Winchester School is on display everywhere the visitor turns. A portrait of the founder dominates the Great Hall; a Memorial Gateway commemorates those former scholars who fell in the Boer War; tablets remind one of the many great men – wardens, teachers or pupils – who have passed through these portals. Yet the place is vital, too, as if it each succeeding generation had been able to adapt to the changing needs of the day and as if, despite the veneration that comes with the passage of time, Saint Mary had not allowed her charge to grow old.

There are many more sights in Winchester than could be covered in the time I had allowed myself: the ancient alms houses at St Cross; the house in College Street where Jane Austen died, having moved to Winchester in the vain hope that the medical treatment she received there would cure her of her ills; and the representation of King Arthur's Round Table which hangs in the Castle Hall. This table was probably made in Tudor times, though it is recorded that Henry VIII entertained the Holy Roman Emperor Charles V in this very hall and apparently believed in the table's authenticity. One recent writer, commenting on this tale, remarked on the 'quaintly attractive, uncritical medieval days when historical perspective was unknown', but went on to muse:

> Yet one may question whether we are really better off because for
> us King Arthur's Round Table has no existence and Arthur himself
> is lost in that weird labyrinth where history and legend, myth and

romance are so strangely and inextricably interwoven; and one turns away baffled and reluctant from many and many an old-world story, and many and many an old-world relic such as this, with the sense of something like a lost inheritance.

While I admit to some sympathy with this view, and did indeed thrill to read the names of Lancelot, Galahad, Bedivere and Kay inscribed round the table as if to mark the places where the knights used to sit, I cannot but agree with the same writer's conclusion:

There is, however, little real excuse for these unavailing regrets in Winchester, for she above all places has store of real history – and such history, too – enough and to spare.

1 July

On leaving Winchester I also, with regret, quitted the banks of the Itchen, and proceeded south-west towards the tiny village of Hursley. Richard Cromwell, Oliver's son and for a short time his successor as Protector of England, was lord of the manor here and buried in the old church. His was a strange career: few people remember that he survived his father not by the few months during which he was nominally in power but by some fifty years, dying at the remarkable age of eighty-six. In fact his father's third son, he had been able to devote the early years of his life to field sports and pleasure, but was thrust into political realms, against his will and against his nature, by the early deaths of his two elder brothers. Reliable records describe him as amiable and popular but weak, and efforts to train him to the work of government came too late.

A mere nine months after the elder Cromwell's death, the country was in

Opposite:

WINCHESTER COLLEGE

The Cloisters
Winchester College Ward
Wilfrid Ball

military and political turmoil; the hapless Richard abdicated, fled abroad a year later when Charles II was restored to the throne and did not return to England for twenty years. The remaining thirty years of his life were spent quietly, largely at Hursley, where he seems to have offended no one.

But the village is really dedicated to the memory of John Keble, who was vicar here for thirty years. Before that he had had an academic career of extraordinary merit at Oxford (where Keble College was later established in his memory); been a founding and prominent member of the Tractarian or Oxford Movement, whose avowed aim was to assert the authority and dignity of the Church of England; and composed that great collection of poetry and hymns, *The Christian Year*. So successful was this work that the restoration of the church at Hursley was funded by the profits therefrom. Keble is buried just outside the church, alongside his wife, who survived him by only six weeks. It is pleasant in the light of this to imagine the domestic bliss which inspired him to pen the lines:

> Sweet is the smile of home; the mutual look
> When hearts are of each other sure;
> Sweet all the joys that crowd the household nook,
> The haunt of all affections pure.

Nor can one fail to be appreciate the piety that moved him to write:

> These eyes, that dazzled now and weak,
> At glancing motes in sunshine wink,
> Shall see the King's full glory break,
> Nor from the blissful vision shrink.

Opposite:

HURSLEY VICARAGE

3 July

And so to Romsey, an ancient market town with an abbey dating in part to Saxon times and much enlarged by the Normans. It is unfair to Romsey to visit it so soon after Winchester, for it is both charming and interesting, but a pale shadow of its larger neighbour. A short stroll outside the town lies Broadlands, the former home of the late Lord Palmerston, a fine eighteenth-century manor whose house and gardens bear the stamp of the great Capability Brown, the man whose sense of mission was so great that he refused a flattering and lucrative offer to go to Ireland on the grounds that he had 'not finished England yet'.

7 July

The poetic mood awakened by Hursley stayed with me until I reached the Isle of Wight, for my purpose there was to visit the home of our late Poet Laureate, Lord Tennyson. He lived at Farringford, on the western end of the island, for forty years and wrote many of his best known poems there. In these days when tourists can visit the island at will – and do so en masse – it seems strange to imagine that what most appealed to him about the house was its seclusion, and that when he first went there in 1853 he and his wife had to cross the Solent by rowing boat.

Tennyson wrote of the place in these lines:

> Should all our churchmen foam in spite
> At you, so careful of the right,
> Yet one lay-hearth would give you welcome
> Take it and come to the Isle of Wight;
>
> Where, far from noise and smoke of town,

Opposite:

ROMSEY HIGH STREET

80

I watch the twilight falling brown
All around a careless-ordered garden
Close to the ridge of a noble down.

You'll have no scandal while you dine,
But honest talk and wholesome wine,
And only hear the magpie gossip
Garrulous under a roof of pine.

Lady Tennyson obviously shared the poet's passion for the place, for she described 'her wild house amongst the pine trees' in these more simple terms:

The golden green of the trees, the burning splendour of Blackgang Chine and the red bank of the primeval river contrasted with the turkish blue of the sea (that is our view from the drawing-room) make altogether a miracle of beauty at sunset. We are glad that Farringford is ours.

I felt glad to have visited it.

10 July

I had no plans to visit seaside resorts on this journey, but I made an exception for Christchurch because no travels around these part of England can be considered complete unless they include the priory here, remarkable for the beauty of its tower and for its great length – it is the largest building of its kind in England. The tower dominates the landscape for several miles around, and the approach to the priory is through a pleasant avenue of elms. The building is a glorious blend of styles, from Saxon to the Renaissance period, and boasts choir stalls older than those in Westminster Abbey. In a sense it is three churches in one: the choir area is the priory church proper, the place of worship for the canons or clergy who live here, and is the only part that should strictly be called 'Christchurch'; the nave is the parish

LORD TENNYSON'S HOME ON THE ISLE OF WIGHT

church, dedicated to the Holy Trinity; and the Lady Chapel forms the manorial church.

Christchurch the town is as ancient as Romsey and Winchester, being one of the 'burghs' or fortified towns built by Alfred the Great to defend his lands against the Danes. Its earlier name was Twyneham or Tweoxna, which might have meant 'the two towns' – perhaps differentiating between the fortified area and the religious establishment. A monastery may have existed here as early as the tenth century, and the Domesday Book refers to Christchurch (which it calls Thuinam) as 'the Monk's Town'. But the priory as we know it was founded by a minister of William II known as Ranulf Passe-Flambard or Pass-the-Torch. Ranulf was notoriously ambitious and self-serving, full of schemes for his own enrichment. Yet to his energies we owe not only this magnificent building but the cathedral at Durham too. As a recent writer put it, 'His motives may have been mixed, but let us be grateful for the result'.

15 July

I continued my pursuit of great churches as my journey took me north and west from Christchurch. My first stop was to be Wells, which has perhaps the prettiest of all England's cathedrals. As I approached the city I was put in mind of W. H. Hudson's experience of the same walk, though at a different time of the year:

> The road I followed from Shepton to Wells winds by the water-side, a tributary of the Brue, in a narrow valley with hills on either side. It is a five-mile road through a beautiful country, where there is practically no cultivation, and the green hills, with brown woods in their hollows, and here and there huge masses of grey and reddish Bath stone cropping out on their sides, resembling gigantic castles and ramparts, long ruined and overgrown with ivy and

Opposite:

CHRISTCHURCH QUAY

bramble, produce the effect of a land dispeopled and gone back to a state of wildness.

A thaw had come that morning, ending the severest frost experienced that winter anywhere in England, and the valley was alive with birds, happy and tuneful at the end of January as in April. Looking down on the stream the sudden glory of a kingfisher passed before me; but the sooty-brown water-ouzel with his white bib, a haunter, too, of this water, I did not see. Within a mile or so of Wells I overtook a small boy who belonged there, and had been to Shepton like me, noticing the birds. 'I saw a kingfisher,' I said. 'So did I,' he returned quickly, with pride. He described a biggish bird, but its colour was not blue – oh, no! I suggested that it was a heron, a long-necked creature under six feet high, of no particular colour. No, it was not a heron; and taking thought, he said, 'I think it was a wild duck.'

Bestowing a penny to encourage him in his promising researches into the feathered world, I went on by a footpath over a hill, and as I mounted to the higher ground there before me rose the noble tower of St Cuthbert's Church, and a little to the right of it, girt with high trees, the magnificent pile of the cathedral, with green hills and the pale sky beyond. O joy to look again on it, to add yet one more enduring image to the number I had long treasured! For the others were not exactly like this one; the building was not looked at from the same point of view at the same season and late hour with the green hills lit by the departing sun and the clear pale winter sky beyond.

Coming in by the moated palace I stood once more on the Green before that west front, beautiful beyond all others, in spite of the strange defeatures Time has written on it. I watched the daws, numerous as ever, still at their old mad games, now springing into

WELLS PALACE

the air to scatter abroad with ringing cries, only to return the next minute and fling themselves back on their old perches on a hundred weather-stained broken statues in the niches.

The ecclesiastical history of Wells dates back at least to the eighth century; the fifteenth bishop was in place at the time of the Conquest. However, the sixteenth, John de Villula, chose to have his see at Bath, because the latter was walled and thus afforded more protection in those troubled times. De Villula paid Henry I £500 for the city, including the abbey, which he subsequently entirely rebuilt. Thereafter the rivalry between Bath and Wells grew to such an extent that in the middle of the twelfth century it was decided that the see should in future be called Bath *and* Wells, and that the bishop should be elected jointly by the monks of Bath and the canons of Wells.

16 July

Bath Abbey was founded in the reign of King Offa of Mercia in the eighth century and witnessed the coronation of Edgar, first king of all England, in the tenth. We owe most of the present building, in the Perpendicular style, to a fifteenth-century bishop named Oliver King, who had a dream in which angel voices revealed to him that the abbey should be restored by a king – which he took, because of his name, to refer to himself. It has been damaged, repaired, extended and restored many times since, most recently and substantially through the work of Sir Gilbert Scott.

Although the abbey is admirable, Bath to me is first and foremost Aquae Sulis, the Roman spa, and secondly the fashionable Regency resort in which Jane Austen set parts of her novels.

The legend of the healing powers of Bath's waters predates the Romans by several centuries. In about 500 BC, Prince Bladud, stricken with leprosy, had been deprived of his honours and forced – because of the extreme horror in which his malady was held – to scrape a living as a roving swineherd. He wandered as far as the present site of Bath, where he observed that his pigs

emerged from a wallow cured of the ailments that had previously afflicted them. Plunging himself into the same mud, he was immediately cleansed of his leprosy and able to return to court, where he claimed his rightful place. Bladud is said to have been the father of King Lear, but as the only 'historical' record of Lear himself is found in the works of Geoffrey of Monmouth, whose chronicles give us also a detailed account of the life of King Arthur, it is perhaps unwise to place too much reliance on this engaging tale.

Whatever the truth of the early history of Bath may be, it is certain that the area was famed for its warm springs by the time the Romans reached it in the first century BC. They established England's first spa resort, building not only the baths but probably a theatre and a gymnasium as well. The baths were dedicated to Minerva, and eighteenth-century workmen found a gilded head of the goddess while digging a sewer in the streets of the city.

The baths were a complex arrangement, originally consisting of a warm, covered swimming pool and two smaller, cooler pools; later additions were a cold room or *frigidarium* with a plunge pool; and two heated rooms, the *tepidarium* and the *caldarium*, kept at different temperatures. The baths were fed by a natural spring producing some 250,000 gallons of water a day at a temperature of about 115° Fahrenheit.

Bath, though not a large city, is pleasantly full of bustle, and though I was fortunate to find it on a brighter day than did Anne Elliot in *Persuasion*, yet I could not help but share the views of her companion; though Anne 'persisted in a very determined, though very silent, disinclination for Bath', Lady Russell felt differently:

> When Lady Russell, not long afterwards, was entering Bath, on a wet afternoon, and driving through the long course of streets from the Old Bridge to Camden Place, amidst the dash of other carriages, the heavy rumble of carts and drays, the bawling of newsmen,

muffin-men, and milkmen, and the ceaseless clink of pattens, she made no complaint. No, these were noises which belonged to the winter pleasures; her spirits rose under their influence; and…she was feeling…that after being long in the country nothing could be so good for her as a little quiet cheerfulness.

It was sympathy with this view that took me to the Pump Room, where fashionable Bath residents and valetudinarians have gathered for generations, to drink the waters and to take comfort in their very nastiness – like 'warm flat-irons', as Dickens' Sam Weller has it – for one cannot but feel that something so unpleasant must be doing one good.

So I ended my brief sojourn in the West Country, the summer weather making my journey even more enjoyable. I am on my way home now and I hope the heat in London will not be too oppressive. My young nephew is to spend a couple of weeks with me. John is such a sensible boy! Especially since the death of my dear wife, I have come to regard him as the son we never had. I do look forward to spoiling him a little and tell him of the many wondrous things I observed over\ the last few months. I also long for the calm atmosphere of my study. I understand that the parcel of new books I ordered has been delivered and I can hardly wait to get home and open it.

I am sure these few weeks at home will make the next leg of my journey that much more rewarding. I have already planned my next excursion from London which will take me to the county that resounds perhaps more than any other in England with the voices of history and literature.

18 August

As anyone with a love of literature must, I started my journey through Warwickshire in Stratford. It has always been a source of wonder to me that so little is known of the life of our greatest playwright; but I found now that while little is known as fact, much is surmised and disputed over,

and views on various aspects of his career are held the more strongly for being without foundation.

William Shakespeare was born on 23 April 1564 – or at least he was christened on the 26th, and it was the common practice of the period to baptise children when they were three days old. His father, John Shakespeare, the son of a farmer, was a well-to-do burgher and had been married for six or seven years to Mary Arden, who had already borne him two daughters who died in infancy. Mary was the daughter of John's father's landlord, but if the Ardens were of gentle birth, the Shakespeares could trace their ancestry back a hundred years and had the distinction of having fought at the Battle of Bosworth. The poet, in other words, was born into a comfortable middle-class home. Of his childhood we know almost nothing, nor of the period between his marriage, of which I shall write more shortly, and his arrival in London, which falls outside the scope of my journey. We do know that John Shakespeare fell on hard times when William was about eleven; but of how the young Shakespeare acquired his love of the theatre and his unsurpassed feeling for the language, there is no inkling.

However he began his career as a writer, there is apparently no basis for the tradition that he wrote the verse about eight nearby villages which begins:

> Piping Pebworth, Dancing Marston,
> Haunted Hillborough, Hungry Grafton,
> Dodging Exhall, Papist Wixford,
> Beggarly Broom and Drunken Bidford...

Whether he wrote it or not, a number of the villages named are connected with the Bard. Temple Grafton is the "hungry" Grafton of the rhyme, so

Opposite:

Anne Hathaway's Cottage

94

called because of the poverty of its soil, and it is here that Shakespeare is said to have married Anne Hathaway. Sadly, the church in which the ceremony would have taken place was pulled down in 1875, so there is nothing but the site to attract the literary pilgrim. If a questioning mind wonders why the wedding should have taken place some miles away from the home of either bride or groom, it is answered by the surmise that both parties wished to keep the wedding a secret. They may also have been staying with relatives of one or other of them at the time.

Tradition also has it that some form of marriage ceremony between Shakespeare and Anne Hathaway took place at Luddington, some four miles from Stratford and six from Temple Grafton. This may have taken the form of a solemn betrothal or 'hand-fasting', morally if not legally binding, and preceded the church ceremony by some time. But the old church at Luddington has also been pulled down and its register has long since vanished, so there exists no documentary record to settle the matter.

The only official record is of a bond issued at Worcester in November 1582, licensing the couple to be married after only one proclamation of banns. The religious ceremony or ceremonies certainly took place after this date, although the next date of which we can be certain is of the christening of Shakespeare's daughter Susanna as early as May 1583, which may explain some of the mystery and the haste.

Anne's paternal home at Shottery still remains, a timber-framed structure with the panels between the timbers filled in with wattle and daub. This cottage, with its rustic garden and ancient well, gives us an idea of what it must have been like in Shakespeare's day, and we can imagine him sitting on the oak settle, conjuring up the ideas that gave us Juliet and Viola, Shylock and Lear. It is one of the very few relics of this period that it is possible to envisage in its original state.

Travelling southward from Temple Grafton one approaches Bidford, where,

about three-quarters of a mile from the village, stands a young crab-apple tree said to have sprung from the ancient one known as 'Shakespeare's Crab Tree'. Here the Bard is supposed to have slept off the effects of a drinking contest in 'drunken Bidford'. However, this new young tree is much closer to the road than the old one, which makes it unlikely that it is a direct descendant. The existence of the Bidford Association of Topers, who were in the habit of challenging their neighbours to tests of endurance in ale-drinking, is first recorded in 1794, so the suggestion that Shakespeare took part in such a bout must, unfortunately, also be regarded as dubious.

21 August

Between Stratford and Warwick lies Baddesley Clinton, a typical old moated manor house, but one of exquisite beauty, and the more interesting because so few of these old fortified dwellings have survived the burden of time and the threat of fire.

The lover of Shakespeare cannot visit here without recalling Mariana of the Moated Grange, now best remembered through the more recent work of Lord Tennyson, but first brought to our notice in *Measure for Measure*:

> Take, oh take, those lips away,
> That so sweetly were forsworn

sings Mariana when she learns of her lover's treachery; or, in the words of Lord Tennyson:

> Unlifted was the clinking latch;
> Weeded and worn the ancient thatch
> Upon the lonely moated grange.
> She only said, 'My life is dreary,
> He cometh not,' she said.

There are many in Warwickshire who regard Baddesley Clinton as *the*

moated grange, the one that inspired Shakespeare to lodge the deserted but loving heart of Mariana there. Certainly Shakespeare spent part of his youth in this area, and his father is known to have been born at nearby Snitterfield. The giant trees which yet stand here in gaunt majesty formed part of the primeval forest of Arden, and one could hope to spy the melancholy Jacques or playful Rosalind from *As You Like It* beneath their shade. Strangely, too, there is mention of an Isabel Shakespeare, living in the nearby nunnery in 1504, in a surviving register.

22 August

And so to Warwick. The traveller with an ear for history could spend many days here, where the castle alone is full of stories to hold him spellbound for as long as he chooses. The history of the castle and the town are closely interwoven and may be said to have begun in 914 when, according to tradition, the Lady Ethelfled of Mercia, daughter of Alfred the Great, built a fortress here. The only surviving trace of it is the mound on which it stood; everything else has long since vanished.

Although Ethelfled's reputation as a castle builder is considerable – to her are attributed many other fortifications in this part of the country, including those at Tamworth and at Stafford – some historians believe that there is more of legend than of fact in her founding of Warwick Castle. She certainly, these doubters concede, added to it and strengthened it, but a fortress of sorts has probably existed on this site since the time of St Dubritius, in the fifth or sixth century. But whatever may be the truth of the matter, the great mound at the northern end of the castle still bears the name of the Mercian princess.

The earls of Warwick and their castle, have frequently played a pivotal role in the relationship between king and nobles, particularly in those long years of war when the barons tried to wrest from their monarch some of his absolute powers. The first Earl of Warwick, a Norman named Henry de Newburgh, fought at Hastings, alongside his elder brother Robert. (The latter became

Earl of Leicester and was great-grandfather to Simon de Montfort, who led the rising against Henry III that is known as the Second Barons' War and for a brief period became virtual ruler of England.) In the reign of King Stephen, Gundreth, widow of Roger de Newburgh, drove the king's soldiers from the castle and surrendered it to the Duke of Normandy, who, after Stephen's death in 1154, came to the throne as Henry II. A little later, during the Barons' War, William de Mauduit, who became Earl of Warwick by virtue of his marriage to a daughter of the Newburgh line, took the part of the king against the barons; his castle was besieged and captured by Sir John Gifford, governor of Kenilworth, and all but the towers destroyed.

It must have been rapidly restored, for two years later Henry III made it his headquarters whilst he was gathering together forces with which to besiege Kenilworth. I shall talk more of the Great Siege of Kenilworth when I reach that town.

Under Henry's successor, Edward I, the then earl, Guy de Beauchamp, repaired and further strengthened Warwick Castle. His name – and his nickname, 'The Black Dog of Arden' – have come down to us because of the role he played in the career of Piers Gaveston, the favourite of Edward II.

Chronicles of the time give us a vivid – if perhaps improbable – picture of Gaveston:

> His features were cast in the finest classic mould. His eyes were dark, soft and lustrous, so was his hair which clustered in thick waxing masses over his broad intellectual forehead. But the great charm of his God-like countenance after all was in his sweet expression, especially when his smile was brightened by the display of an even set of teeth as white as egg-shells. Witty, brave

Opposite:

BADDESLEY CLINTON HILL

102

and highly accomplished, with the most irresistibly pleasing manners, he had likewise a colossal figure, towering high even over the noble forms of tall companions. To these physical advantages were superadded mental endowments of the highest order. Thus gifted with a sparkling and brilliant intellect, Gaveston's mind had been early imbued with all the fascinating charms of the soft and chivalrous literature of the troubadours or minstrels of his native Gascony.

No wonder the young king, who has gone down in history as weak and extravagant, was smitten by such a paragon. Sadly, however...

> ...although so endowed by nature, and by high cultivation, with such singular advantages of a majestic and commanding presence, grace of form and bewitching manners, and so capable of creating the most passionate love and affection for him, [Gaveston] was utterly destitute of those higher qualities which serve to procure lasting esteem and regard. A life of sensual enjoyment and luxurious magnificence was, unhappily, too well suited to the impulsive passions of His Majesty, for he and his friend ran together in couples through every scene of loose intrigue and coarse debauchery.

In a land where the barons now held considerable power, it was possible for them to put an end to the scandal that the king was creating. When remonstrances failed, a number of earls, including Guy of Warwick, contrived to make Parliament banish Gaveston from the kingdom, but the Gascon went first to Bristol and then to Ireland, where Edward made him Lord Deputy and sent him presents. Over the next three years Gaveston was recalled, lavished with gifts (including a table alleged to have belonged to King Arthur, which he sent to Gascony), banished again and once more recalled. In the early summer of 1312 the lords finally took to arms. They besieged Scarborough Castle, where Gaveston was, compelled him to

WARWICK CASTLE

surrender and took him a prisoner to Warwick. Here the royal favourite was tried by torchlight in the great hall and condemned to death by a tribunal of barons led by his implacable enemy, the Earl of Warwick. On the following morning Gaveston was taken to Blacklow Hill, near Guy's Cliff, just outside the town, and there executed. Tradition has it that his head rolled off down the hill into a thicket, where it was picked up by a missionary friar, who carried it away concealed under his hood. Some of the holy brethren came shortly afterwards to collect the body and buried it in their own church; two years later it was removed by the king's orders and reinterred with great pomp at His Majesty's own church at King's Langley. Edward is said to have deposited two palls of cloth of gold on the coffin with his own hands.

Not all of Warwick's history has been so bloody. The castle has entertained many royal guests, including Henry V – who is said to have been received with a state which was extravagant even for the Middle Ages – and Queen Elizabeth on two occasions, with scarcely less magnificence. In 1605, James I granted the castle to Sir Fulke Greville, who found it falling into ruin and spent the then enormous sum of £30,000 in repairing it and fitting it up. He must also have incurred vast expenses by his entertainment of James I, who graced the castle with his presence on no fewer than four different occasions.

During the Civil War, Sir Fulke's successor, Robert Greville (later Lord Brooke), took the Parliamentary side, as a result of which the castle and inhabitants of Warwick were again at the centre of tumult. In 1642, when its master was from home, the place was besieged by royalist troops and gallantly defended by its governor, Sir Edward Peyton. He hung out two flags, one plain red and the other bearing a red cross, in defiance of the Catholics, and later when his adversaries were attempting to starve the garrison out, hung out a device of a Bible and a winding-sheet, to show that, while he was trusting in God to deliver him, he was not afraid of Death.

Since those days the castle has remained the peaceful residence of the Greville family, who have at various times entertained royalty in the persons of

William III, George IV whilst Prince Regent, Queen Adelaide, Queen Victoria and the Prince Consort.

26 August

Having drunk my fill of history, I took myself for a ramble a little more than a mile to the north of Warwick, on the Coventry Road, to Guy's Cliffe. Now the seat of the Percy family, it is beautifully situated, surrounded by trees and overlooking a particularly lovely stretch of the Avon. In antiquity the place was known as Gibbclyve, and it remained so until the fifteenth century, when the legendary exploits of Guy of Warwick made him such a popular hero that his name was intertwined with that of this ancient place. Sadly, it seems likely that Guy's adventures belong to an earlier time – probably the Age of Chivalry that surrounded the Crusades – and there is no record of him in any reliable mediaeval chronicle.

The setting of the mansion, itself architecturally commonplace, is as picturesque as any I have seen. It is built on a sandstone cliff overhanging the river, which widens into a large pool in front of the house. The cliff is honeycombed with caves and hollows, both natural and man-made, and the grounds are charming. Across the pool stands what is known as the Saxon Mill – an attractive building, though not as old as one might have hoped. There is known to have been a mill on this site in Saxon times, but the existing one is a much later replacement.

If Guy's Cliffe cannot boast romantic associations with Guy of Warwick, it can claim to have played a part in the love affair of young Sarah Kemble, who become famous as the great tragic actress Mrs. Siddons. Sarah's father, Robert Kemble, another great name from the theatre of his day, ran a theatrical company, and Sarah had fallen in love with a fellow actor, William Siddons. Kemble clearly disapproved of this connection and, with a view to separating the young couple, accepted an offer from Lady Mary Greatheed of Guy's Cliffe, whom they had met while performing at Warwick, that Sarah should stay with the wealthy widow as a companion. Like many such

ruses, it failed lamentably, for less than a year later, in November 1773, William and Sarah were married at Coventry. Lady Mary approved of the match or had been won over, for Sarah Siddons is recorded as having paid several visits to Guy's Cliffe after her marriage.

27 August

To Leamington, not to take the waters or admire the fashionable visitors to this elegant spa, but to see one of the many spots in Warwickshire that are claimed to be the centre of England. Folklore insists that the entire county is worthy of this title, but a number of different localities are specially distinguished. The one near Leamington is an oak tree, standing on a mound by the side of the road. It is certainly a splendid specimen; how much more worthy its claims are than those of its rivals, I am not competent to judge. There is a cross at Meriden which is also said to be the exact centre of the country, but it has been moved in the memory of man, and whether its old or its new site is the point in question seems not to be known.

The Roman centre of England, and probably the one with the strongest claim of all, is situated on the high ground between the counties of Leicester and Warwick, where the Watling Street and Fosse Ways cross each other. This spot, known as High Cross, lies near the Roman station of Bennones, known to the Saxons as Cleaycestre. The shattered remains of a pillar stand in a garden there, on the site of an ancient tumulus. The pillar was erected in the time of Queen Anne in obedience to an order of the Quarter Sessions, because it was again deemed the centre of England. Part of the inscription runs: 'If, traveller, you search for the footsteps of the ancient Romans, here you may behold them, for here their most celebrated ways, crossing one another, extend to the utmost boundaries of Britain.' The ground here is so

Opposite:

GUY'S CLIFFE MILL

high and the surrounding country so low and flat, that it is said that 57 churches may be seen from High Cross without the aid of a glass.

Sad news for the spot near Leamington; though the oak tree is still a fine specimen.

28 August

From Leamington it is but a short walk to Kenilworth, where the castle is a magnificent red sandstone ruin, now overgrown with ivy and crumbling into ever greater decay. But what romance is here! When it was but a century old it came into the hands of Simon de Montfort as part of his wife's dowry. She was Eleanor, Dowager Countess of Pembroke, sister to King Henry III, and de Montfort married her with the king's blessing but in the teeth of strong opposition from the barons. De Montfort was, after all, a foreigner – born in Normandy – and the English nobles viewed with disfavour his rise to prominence and his alliance with the royal family. Ere long, of course, he had won the favour of the barons and fallen out with the king; from which events the history of the English Parliament may be said to have arisen.

The Great Siege of Kenilworth was the culmination of five years and more of hostility between king and nobles over who should have most power in the land. In the summer of 1265 de Montfort held the king a virtual prisoner and, having been fighting in the Welsh Marches, advanced towards Evesham. His son, also Simon, was in charge at Kenilworth. The royalist force was led not by the king but by his son Edward, the future Edward I, who at the age of twenty-five was 'winning his spurs' in his father's cause. The elder de Montfort had planned to join his son before doing battle with the prince, but young Simon had fallen into Edward's hands, along with stores, treasures and many of his knights; the rest were forced to take refuge in Kenilworth, which the prince surrounded in a masterly manner. De Montfort, seeing the end approaching, exclaimed, 'The Lord have mercy on our souls, for I see that our bodies are Prince Edward's.' He fell, sword in hand, at the Battle of

Evesham a few days later. For a while liberty seemed dead and the laws which had been bought so dearly were set at naught, but that same Prince Edward was to prove a more just ruler than his father had been.

It is impossible to visit Kenilworth without thinking of Scott's novel and the mystery of Amy Robsart. Scott's account is entirely fictitious – for the purposes of his narrative he has Amy present at Kenilworth in 1575, when her husband, Robert Dudley, Earl of Leicester, the then owner of the castle, and Queen Elizabeth's favourite, entertained the queen there amid much pomp and splendour. History, however, records that Amy died at Cumnor Place fifteen years before this royal visit.

Robert Dudley married Amy Robsart in 1550, when she was eighteen. The marriage took place at the palace of Sheen in the presence of Edward VI and many of his court. For the next ten years Dudley spent much of his time in attendance at court while his wife lived mostly in the country

On 8 September 1560 Amy was found dead at the foot of a staircase, with her neck broken, by servants returning from Abingdon fair. An inquiry into the circumstances of her death failed to discover any suggestion that another party had been implicated in it.

Although Lord Leicester was undoubtedly secretly married at the time the royal visit to Kenilworth, it was not to Amy Robsart. His marital affairs seem to have been complex, for in 1573 he apparently wed Lady Douglas Sheffield, by whom he had a son, but there seems to be some doubt about the legality of this connection. In 1578, while Lady Douglas Sheffield was still alive, he married the widowed Lettice, Countess of Essex, with whom he had been carrying on an intrigue at the time of the royal visit, when her

Opposite:

KENILWORTH CASTLE

husband too was still living. On his death, Leicester bequeathed Kenilworth to his brother for his lifetime, then to his son by Lady Douglas Sheffield, whom in his will he named Sir Robert Dudley. Legal proceedings between this lad and Lady Lettice prevented the former from proving his legitimacy and, in the early years of the reign of King James I, possession of Kenilworth Castle passed to the crown.

29 August

A good morning's walk from Kenilworth brought me to Coventry, an ancient city of great interest to archaeologists, architects and historians alike. As I approached I was struck by the vast number of church spires that met my gaze; and once in the town I could not but be impressed both by the architecture of these churches and by the quantity of old timbered houses which survive to delight the eye.

Among the many buildings of interest are Ford's Alms-Houses, situated in Grey Friars Lane and founded in 1529 by the will of a local merchant named William Ford, to provide a refuge for the poor. The front of the house is a beautiful and almost unique specimen of timber framework construction, certainly one of the finest of its kind to be found in England. The gables of the roof, the timbers beneath them and the windows over the entrance arch are all elaborately and magnificently carved. Passing through the archway one comes to an inner courtyard around which are situated the rooms of the almswomen. No student of the domestic architecture of the sixteenth century should overlook such a fine example of the art and craft of that period.

The name Coventry is generally thought to derive from the word Conventry or 'convent town', although some attribute it to the River Cune, the Celtic name for the Sherbourne, on which the city stands. In any case, Coventry

Opposite:

COVENTRY HIGH STREET

was probably founded by the Britons, and Canute is said to have destroyed a nunnery here when he invaded Mercia in 1016.

Later the same century Leofric, Earl of Mercia, and his countess, the famous Godiva, founded a Benedictine monastery on the site of the original Saxon nunnery of St Osburg, and very richly endowed it. Godiva is said to have searched the country for 'skilful goldsmiths, who, with all the gold and silver she had, made crosses, images of saints, and other curious ornaments, which she devoutly disposed thereto'.

It is around this Lady Godiva or Godeva that the best known legend of Coventry centres. The tale of her ride through the town may well be apocryphal, for the first description of it is to be found in the writings of Roger of Wendover, a chronicler of the early twelfth century – almost a century after it is supposed to have taken place. It should also be recorded that Roger had a tendency towards romance which occasionally left his facts open to question. That said, this is how he relates the legend:

> The Countess Godiva, who was a great lover of God's mother, longing to free the town of Coventry from the oppression of a heavy toll, and even with urgent prayers besought her husband, with every regard to Jesus Christ and His mother, he would free the town from that service, and from all other heavy burdens; and when the Earl sharply rebuked her for foolishly asking what was so much to his damage he always forbade her for evermore to speak to him on the subject; and while she, on the other hand, with a woman's pertinacity, never ceased to exasperate her husband with that matter, he at last made her this answer:

Opposite:

Fords Hospital, Coventry

'Mount your horse and ride naked before all the people, through the market of the town from one end to the other, and on your return you shall have your request.'

To which Godiva replied, 'But will you give me permission if I am willing to do it?'

'I will,' said he.

Whereupon the Countess, beloved of God, loosed her hair and let down her tresses, which covered the whole of her body like a veil, and then mounting her horse and attended by two knights she rode through the market-place without being seen, except her fair legs; and having completed the journey, she returned with gladness to her astonished husband, and obtained of him what she had asked, for Earl Leofric freed the town of Coventry and its inhabitants from the aforesaid service, and confirmed what he had done by a charter.

Those familiar with the modern version of the Godiva legend will notice that several details are missing from this early account: the suggestion that the people of the town remained indoors out of respect for the countess was not recorded until a further century after Roger of Wendover; while further 'embellishments' such as the story of 'Peeping Tom', whose eyes either fell out or were struck blind as a punishment for his impertinence in spying on her, are a seventeenth-century addition.

1 September
Before concluding my tour in Birmingham, I took myself to Berkswell, which

Opposite:

PALACE YARD, COVENTRY

lies equidistant between the city I was leaving and that to which I was bound. The reason for this detour was the reputation of the well near the churchyard, which is said to have been used for the purposes of baptism and immersion.

There are many strange and ancient beliefs attached to wells in Warwickshire. Many are sanctified and dedicated to various saints and many more have miraculous virtues attributed to them. Sketchley Well is supposed to have the power of sharpening the wits of those who drink its waters. There was also formerly an ancient well by the Whitnash brook of which it is said that the ancient inhabitants, when removing the bell from their old church to its present site, brought it to the holy well to be freshly consecrated. In doing so, they accidentally dropped it in the water, where it disappeared. The country people who wish to know coming events cast stones into the well at night, and in the morning their questions are answered by the sounding of the bell. The site is now drained, but the little stream which flows into the brook is still believed to be possessed of healing power and people come from great distances to procure the water.

2 September

As the afternoon wore on I was pleased to see my cousins' house in the outskirts of Birmingham. In the ten years since they moved to this part of the country, and despite many kind invitations, it is my first visit. I have to admit that pleasant as my walks have been over the last few months, the tiredness I feel makes me realise the passing of the years. The weather which had remained so warm for the time of the year, seemed to break abruptly yesterday. I was drenched and arrived at the house thoroughly chilled. My cousin and his wife scolded and fussed over me in the most friendly manner and I look forward to a few days of cossetting before returning to my own house. Before I do so, however, I intend to visit Birmigham.

Little is known of its early history, except that it was a market town prior to the Norman Conquest and that fairs were held here very early on in its existence. There is no mention in the Domesday Book of there being any

BERKSWELL

church in Birmingham, but when St Martin's was being rebuilt in 1562, some stonework, hundreds of years old, was discovered, suggesting that there had been a church on that site in Saxon times. The Old Cross nearby was almost certainly the ancient centre of the town.

But it is not history that one seeks in Birmingham. Compared with Stratford, Warwick or Coventry it seems both prosaic and commercial. Amid the general air of wealth and industry, as one admires the fine streets and handsome public buildings of more recent years, it is difficult to imagine that in the sixteenth century the houses would have resembled those of Chester or Shrewsbury. Set in a county devoted almost exclusively to romance and legend, this city is a celebration of modern prosperity.

I can only give thanks to God that 1901 which started so mournfully with the passing of Her Majesty, Queen Victoria, brought me so many varied experiences and fascinating encounters. Where better to end my walking tour than in this place which encourages one to look forward?

ACKNOWLEDGEMENTS

The pictures in this book are the work of the following artists:
Helen Allingham: pages 19 and 83.
Wilfrid Ball: pages 9, 21, 23, 25, 27, 29, 31, 33, 35, 37, 39, 41, 43, 45, 57, 49, 51, 53, 67, 69, 71, 73, 75, 77, 79, 81, 85 and endpapers.
Sutton Palmer: pages 11, 13, 15, 17, 55, 57, 59, 61, 63 and 65.
Walter Tyndale: pages 87, 89, 91 and 95.
Fred Whitehead: 95, 97, 99, 101, 103, 105, 107, 109, 111, 113, 115, 117, 119, 121, 123, 125.and frontispiece.

St Martin's Church, Birmingham